Teddy Bear Redwork

Jan Rapacz

C&T PUBLISHING

© 2003, Jan Rapacz
Editor-in-Chief: Darra Williamson
Editor and Technical Editor: Ellen Pahl
Copyeditor: Katrina Lamken
Proofreader: Carol Barrett
Cover Designer: Christina D. Jarumay
Book Designer: Staci Harpole, Cubic Design
Design Director: Diane Pedersen
Illustrator: Kirstie L. McCormick
Production Assistant: Luke Mulks and Kristy A. Konitzer
Room Setting Photographer and Stylist: Diane Pedersen
Bear Handlers: Kristy A. Konitzer and Diane Pedersen
Quilt Photographer: Sharon Risedorph

Published by C&T Publishing, Inc., P.O. Box 1456,
Lafayette, California 94549

Rapacz, Jan
  Teddy bear redwork: 25 fresh, new designs, step-by-
step projects, quilts and more / Jan Rapacz.
    p. cm.
  ISBN 1-57120-221-8 (paper trade)
  1. Patchwork--Patterns 2. Embroidery--Patterns.
  3. Redwork. 4. Patchwork quilts. 5. Teddy bears in art.
  I. Title.
  TT835.R343 2003
  746.46'041--dc21
                              2002155211

Printed in China
10 9 8 7 6 5 4 3 2 1

ACKNOWLEDGMENTS

I extend my thanks and gratitude to the editors
at C&T Publishing, who turn creative ideas into
wonderful books.

Special thanks also go to: The C&T staff for the use
of their teddy bears; Carol and John Barrett for the use
of their home for the styled photographs; Joe and
Susan Steffen of The Steffen Collection Antiques and
Collectibles for the use of the toy wagon; Kerry
Hansing for the use of her antique sewing supplies and
toy sewing machine; Sheila Pedersen for the use of her
family heirloom linens and sewing supplies.

FOREWORD

What little girl doesn't remember skipping rope to
the rhyme "Teddy Bear, Teddy Bear"? And who doesn't
have a memory of a favorite bear from childhood?
This book is for everyone with a happy teddy bear
memory, as well as today's needleworkers and teddy
bear collectors.

This book is dedicated to my family, who
are always enthusiastic about my projects—
even when they have to eat pizza three
times a week.

CONTENTS

WHAT IS REDWORK?

Redwork is quite simply embroidery that is stitched using red thread. It evolved from the resurgence of detailed surface embroidery in the mid-to-late-1800s, the Victorian era, which was also the heyday of elaborate crazy quilts. It did not come into its own, in the style that we know it now, however, until the early 1900s. At that time, "penny squares" became popular. Penny squares were line embroidery designs that were drawn in quilt-block sizes. They could easily be traced from the pages of a magazine, or could be purchased individually for a penny each. Often, the completed blocks were traded, shared, and made into friendship quilts. Penny squares were almost always stitched in a floss color called "turkey red." At the time, turkey red was the only color that was reliably colorfast and readily available.

Redwork's charm lies in its simplicity. Primarily executed in outline stitch, the most basic of embroidery stitches, **it is quick to learn and quite easy to master**. The first chapters in the book provide the stitching instructions and list the minimal tools and materials that you need. The result of just a little practice with a needle, embroidery floss, and fabric is a heartwarming, vintage look that evokes the feeling of simpler times.

I originally designed the teddy bear patterns in this book with a children's storybook in mind. I gave them a slightly more up-to-date look than traditional vintage patterns. I think it adds freshness, yet still retains the charm of original vintage designs. These designs are readily adaptable to contemporary quilts and accessory projects. Look through the book at the quilts, accessory projects, and the suggested adaptations. Select your favorite designs, then sit back and relax with needle and thread. **Enjoy your stitching!**

MATERIALS AND TOOLS

You won't really need a lot of tools to get started with redwork embroidery. It's an easy technique to learn and requires a minimum of supplies along with your usual sewing tools and accessories.

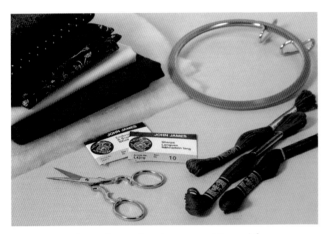

Tools and supplies that you will need for redwork embroidery

Fabric

Always use 100% cotton fabric for redwork embroidery. Polyester blends may wrinkle less, but they are difficult to work with because they resist the penetration of the needle; they also put increased "wear" on the floss as it moves through the fabric.

Embroider on a white or off-white fabric to allow the design to stand out to best advantage. Unbleached muslin is an inexpensive option with a traditional look, but lightweight broadcloth in pure white produces a brighter contrast.

Use 100% cotton fabric for any sashings, borders, and backings. When choosing red fabrics to use in piecing, take a sample of your chosen floss with

you to help coordinate colors. The classic turkey red color may be difficult to keep in your mind's eye when you are confronted with the wide array of red prints at the fabric store.

Test the colorfastness of commercially dyed fabrics. Before pre-washing, cut a small scrap of your chosen fabric. Immerse the scrap in a bowl of clean, hot water. Agitate by hand for a few minutes, then remove the scrap. Look closely at the water. If the water is even slightly pink, the fabric will bleed when it is washed. Consider using a different fabric.

After testing for colorfastness, always machine wash and dry the fabric to pre-shrink it. If you do not, the embroidery and any piecing may pucker when it is washed. Pre-washing also removes any sizing from the fabric, making it softer and easier to work with. Press the washed and dried fabric before using it.

Batting

Most redwork quilts are only lightly quilted; that is, the spaces between the rows of quilting stitches are quite large. Choose a quilt batting to accommodate this. Polyester batting typically requires less quilting than cotton batting, but there are some cotton battings that can be left unquilted for several inches. Be sure to check the package instructions.

Bear in Mind

A low-loft batting (one that is less "puffy") is usually preferable and will show off the embroidery on your quilt. A high-loft batting tends to obscure the embroidery.

Embroidery Floss

Use six-strand cotton embroidery floss. All of the examples in this book use DMC #321, but several shades are available that look like the traditional turkey red.

Like red fabric, red floss should be tested for colorfastness. Remove the labels from a skein of floss, submerge it in a bowl of hot water, and gently agitate. Remove the floss and look carefully at the water. If the water is pink, the floss will bleed. Rinse the floss repeatedly, until the water remains colorless. If repeated rinsing continues to produce pink water, choose another floss.

Needles

The right needle is very much a personal preference. I like sharps, in sizes 7 through 10. I feel that they have a finer, sharper point that makes it easier for me to produce a fine stitch. But if you have trouble threading a needle, try an embroidery needle, size 7 or 8, as embroidery needles have longer eyes. A higher needle size number indicates a smaller, finer needle. A lower needle size number indicates a longer, thicker needle.

The needle must make a hole in the fabric that is large enough for the floss to pass through without fraying, but small enough to "close up" around the completed stitch. If you find your floss is wearing out before the end of a strand, choose a larger needle. If you find your completed embroidery shows needle holes, choose a smaller needle.

Needles do get damaged and they do wear out. If you feel your needle snagging the fabric or dragging, throw it out. Don't let a bad needle ruin the pleasure of embroidery.

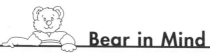

Bear in Mind

Redwork embroidery is done on a single layer of lightweight fabric, so most people do not use a thimble. A thimble may actually hinder your ability to place each stitch accurately, resulting in less fine work. But, do what works for you. If you like using a thimble, use the style that works best for you.

Scissors

Use embroidery scissors, which are smaller than standard sewing shears. Embroidery scissors with curved blades make it easier to cut the floss close to the fabric, but the points can get you into trouble. If you have ever accidentally snipped into the fabric when cutting the floss, you may want to invest in a pair of blunt-end embroidery scissors.

Hoop

An embroidery hoop is essential for smooth, even stitches. Not only will it improve the quality of your work, but it will also save your hand and finger muscles from the tiring work of keeping the fabric taut enough for stitching.

A 5" or 7" diameter hoop works best for most redwork projects. This size allows a fairly large working area, requiring that you move the hoop only a few times to complete a square. With a larger hoop, tension is more difficult to control, and it becomes hard to reach the center of the stitching area.

Many people like wooden hoops, but I think they are risky to use because fabric left in the hoop for any length of time can discolor from the wood. I like the combination plastic and metal, snap-in style hoops.

Regardless of the type of hoop you use, remove the fabric from the hoop whenever you will not be stitching for more than a couple of hours, as the hoop can easily distort the fabric.

Practice putting your fabric into a hoop before you begin embroidering. Getting just the right tension takes some experience. When you think the tension is right, look closely at the threads that make up the weave of the fabric. They should still be perpendicular. If they are not, the fabric has been pulled off-grain, and the stitches will be distorted.

Whenever possible, cut the fabric larger than the final piece needs to be. The larger border of fabric around the embroidered area allows for easier placement in the hoop.

REDWORK EMBROIDERY TECHNIQUES

Once you have the necessary tools and supplies, choose the design that you'd like to stitch. The first step in the embroidery process is to transfer the design from paper onto your fabric.

Enlarging and Reducing Patterns

The designs in this book are given at actual size. You will not need to enlarge them; however, using a photocopy or a tracing on plain white paper will be easier than tracing the patterns from the book. The designs can also be resized to fit many other uses. A copy machine with enlarging and reducing capabilities makes this process easy. Your local copy store or printer can provide this service. All the designs in this book may be photocopied in any size for your personal use.

Transferring the Pattern

Once the pattern is the desired size, it needs to be transferred to fabric. Since redwork is done on white fabric, tracing is the easiest method. Lay the fabric over the pattern, and trace the lines. A light box, available at craft stores, will make seeing the lines through the fabric easier. An inexpensive version of a light box is made for children, and is available in the craft department of toy stores for less than $10. A sunny window works, but it never fails that you'll want to transfer a pattern at night. If you have a glass coffee table, you can put a lamp underneath to improvise a light table. In a pinch, I have darkened the lines on my pattern with a black marker, and traced without a light source.

Marking the Design

Whatever instrument you use for marking, it must produce a very fine line, and either wash out entirely, or be entirely permanent (not bleed). I recommend a very sharp pencil with a hard lead. It makes a very fine line, which is completely covered by the embroidery, and washes out cleanly.

"Disappearing" blue or purple ink markers are favored by some, but I find that they produce quite a fat line that is difficult to cover entirely. In addition, the chemicals in some of these pens may cause the lines to reappear as a yellow or brown line years down the road.

Permanent micro-point pens work well for some. I have trouble with these bleeding, both as they mark, and later when they are washed.

Other options are carbon paper, and the similar, waxy transfer paper. They are placed over the fabric, and transfer pigment to the fabric when you write on the paper. They tend to smudge onto white fabric, so I use them only when the fabric is too heavy to see through for tracing.

Centering the Design

I generally tend to "eyeball" my designs when centering, rather than measuring precisely. Since some of the designs are slightly asymmetrical in themselves, I feel that placing them so that they are slightly off-center is actually more visually pleasing and tends to balance the asymmetry of the embroidery design. However, there are crosshatch marks in the patterns so that you can center the design exactly if you prefer.

To center a design on your fabric, fold the fabric in half and make a crease in the center. Fold it in half in the opposite direction and make another small crease in the center. Line this center point up with the crosshatch mark of the pattern when tracing. Mark the center point very lightly with pencil and use that later on when trimming and squaring up blocks.

The Embroidery Stitches

There's no reason to be intimidated by embroidery stitching. In redwork, there are only two basic stitches that are easy to learn: the outline stitch and the French knot.

Cut the floss into 18" lengths. Longer lengths will fray and frizz from being pulled through the fabric too often before they are used up. All of the projects in this book use two strands of the six-strand floss. Always "strip" the floss before threading your needle: After cutting an 18" length, separate each of the six strands. Then, combine two of the individual strands back together for use. Using multiple strands without completely separating them first will produce embroidery that is uneven, bumpy, and of varying thickness.

Outline Stitch

The outline stitch is the primary stitch used in redwork. This stitch alone accomplishes 95% of the embroidery designs in this book. The outline stitch is also sometimes called the stem stitch. The line of stitching proceeds from left to right. The needle goes through the fabric from right to left, and each stitch overlaps approximately half of the previous stitch.

1. To start, bring the needle up at A. With the floss hanging below the stitching line, insert the needle down at B and up at C. Pull the floss through.

Begin at A, insert the needle at B,
and bring it up again at C.

2. To continue, insert the needle down at D and up at E. E is very close to, but not in the same hole as B. Pull the floss through.

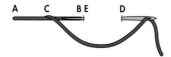

Insert the needle down at D and up at E.

3. Repeat step 2 for the entire line of stitching.

Continue with evenly spaced stitches.

Bear in Mind

Always keep the thread below your needle for nice, even stitches.

French Knot

French knots are used wherever there is a dot on the pattern. They make perfect periods for the end of sentences, they dot the letter *i*, and create wonderful texture and dimension as well.

1. Bring the needle up at A, where the French knot is needed. Wrap the floss around the needle twice. (A traditional French knot has only one wrap, but I find that two wraps help prevent the knot from pulling out and make the finished knot stand up nicely, adding more dimension.)

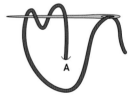

Wrap the floss around the needle twice.

2. Hold the floss taut, so the wraps stay fairly tight around the needle, and insert the needle back down at B. B is close to, but not in the same hole as A. Hold the wrapped floss down close to the fabric, and pull the needle through to the back of the fabric.

Insert the needle down at B.

Polishing Your Technique

Once you've mastered the basic stitches, read on to learn the finer points of embroidery for your projects to be most successful and pleasing.

Beginning and Ending

Avoid knots when beginning and ending a strand of floss, as they cause bumps in the finished work.

1. To start the first strand, bring the needle up, leaving a tail of 3" to 4". Stitch as usual, being careful on the first few stitches not to pull the floss out of the fabric.

2. Stitch until 3" to 4" of the floss remain. Bring the needle to the back of the fabric. Weave the remaining floss through several of the stitches on the back of the fabric, without piercing the fabric. Trim off the excess tail.

3. Thread the original tail into the needle. Weave the tail into the back of the stitches from the beginning of that strand of floss, without piercing the fabric. After weaving through several stitches, trim off the excess tail.

Traveling Stitches

Traveling stitches are those stitches that carry the floss from one location to another on the back of the work. Because the floss is red and the fabric is white, long traveling stitches tend to shadow through when looking at the front of the work. In addition, traveling stitches can cause the fabric to pull out of shape.

Limit traveling stitches as much as possible. In most cases, it is better to end a strand and start another one, as described above. Traveling stitches up to $1/2$" long are usually acceptable.

Beginning Again

When starting a new length of thread in a long continuous line of stitching, begin on the back of the fabric. Weave the needle through the last several stitches of the previous strand without piercing the fabric. Pull the floss through until the tail of the floss is buried in the stitching. While making the first few stitches, be careful not to pull the floss out of the fabric.

Keeping Your Work Clean

Keeping your work clean as you stitch eliminates the need to wash the embroidered piece before incorporating it into your project. Follow these tips to avoid laundering as much as possible.

- *Always wash your hands before you begin to stitch.*
- *In warm weather, wash your hands frequently when stitching, as perspiration can stain your work.*
- *Do not eat or snack while stitching.*
- *When setting your work down for any length of time, put it in a plastic bag, sewing box, or other container to keep off the dust.*
- *Keep your project out of reach of children and pets.*

Pressing

Once the embroidery design is complete, press the fabric to remove wrinkles caused by the hoop. Place a white terrycloth towel on the ironing board. Place the completed embroidery right side down on the towel. Press the back of the embroidered piece carefully, using the nap of the towel to protect the texture of the right side of the embroidery. Use a dry iron on the cotton setting.

Bear in Mind

If your fabric has become stretched or distorted, you can use a bit of steam to gently ease it back into a perfect square.

CARE AND DISPLAY OF REDWORK

Cleaning Redwork

In theory, a properly constructed redwork project can be machine washed on the gentle cycle. I have never been able to do this, however. After the hours of loving labor spent on a project, I just can't trust it to the machine.

Whether you hand or machine wash, use cold water and a mild, nonchlorine detergent. Agitate gently, and do not wring.

Rinsing is the most important part of the washing process. Any detergent left in the project will discolor it over time. Rinse with cold water for longer than you think is required. Then rinse some more.

While I never machine wash my projects, I sometimes use the machine spin cycle to remove the water. This avoids the temptation to wring out the water, which can seriously distort the fabric and embroidery. If you're not using a machine spin, drain and push out as much water as possible without twisting.

Spread the project out flat on a clean white towel or sheet to air dry. Do not hang the item to dry, as this will pull the fabric and embroidery out of shape. Dry the project out of direct sunlight to prevent fading.

After the quilt is completely dry, put it in a dryer, on a non-heat setting, for 10 minutes to fluff it up. For non-quilted items, a touch-up pressing of the fabric around the embroidery may be required. Follow the pressing instructions on page 9.

Storage

To store a redwork project, roll or fold it carefully. Fold so that the center of an embroidered area remains flat and unfolded. Folds in the design area can be difficult to press out.

When storing redwork projects for any extended period, the enemy is acid. Any acidity in the materials surrounding the project will cause the whites to turn yellow or brown. Paper that is not labeled "acid free" or "archival quality" will contain acid. Do not store any project wrapped in acidic paper of any kind.

A safer option is to wrap a clean, white, 100% cotton sheet, towel, or pillowcase around the project to protect it from dust and other soil, without exposing it to acid.

A cedar chest, the traditional storage place for embroidered linens, is actually not a great place to store these kinds of projects, as the wood releases acid and other chemicals that will discolor the fabric over time.

Bear in Mind

A general rule of thumb is that your projects will like conditions that you like. A storage area that feels hot or damp to you will damage your project over time.

Display

Ideally, redwork projects should be displayed, not hidden away somewhere in storage. To preserve their original condition, however, take care in the way they are displayed.

As in storing the projects, avoid contact with acidic materials. If the completed project will be matted and framed, use archival quality products.

Quilts are often displayed by hanging them on the wall. Do not hang a quilt only by the upper corners. The weight will pull the quilt out of shape. Use a quilt hanger that runs across the length of the upper edge. Or, create a hanging sleeve or rod pocket; see below.

Avoid displaying your projects in prolonged direct sunlight, as they will fade. Dust any exposed fabric frequently to avoid permanent soiling.

Adding a Hanging Sleeve

If you want the option of hanging your quilt on the wall, make a simple hanging sleeve or rod pocket.

1. *Cut a piece of fabric that is 8" wide by the finished width of your quilt.*
2. *Fold the short edges of the rectangle under ¹/₂" and press. Fold under another ¹/₂" and press.*
3. *Fold the rectangle in half lengthwise, with right sides together. Stitch the long raw edges together, creating a long tube or sleeve. Turn the sleeve right side out, and press the seam open.*
4. *Center the seam and press the sleeve flat.*
5. *With the seam facing the backing of the quilt, center and pin the sleeve to the back of the quilt along the top edge. Hand sew the sleeve to the quilt.*
6. *Run a dowel or curtain rod through the sleeve and hang the quilt.*

Labeling

Often, redwork projects are given as gifts. Include a note or add a label to the project with care instructions, so the receiver will know how to keep the gift in beautiful condition. And add a label that includes your name, date, hometown, and any other relevant information to document your handcrafted item.

A Special Quilt Label

Always add a label to your quilts to document where, when, and by whom a quilt was made. The perfect crowning touch for an embroidered redwork quilt is a label done in the same fashion. I've included a pattern below.

1. *Cut a rectangle of white fabric, 8" x 12". Enlarge and transfer the label design to the fabric; include your own name and date.*
2. *Embroider the design and press.*
3. *Trim the fabric to 6" x 10". Turn the raw edges under ¹/₄" and press. Hand stitch the label to the lower right corner of the back of the quilt, being careful not to stitch through to the front of the quilt.*

Pattern for quilt label. Enlarge 225%.

Read all instructions before beginning. • *Fabric and yardage estimates in the materials list are based on a 40" width of useable fabric to allow for fraying and any shrinking from laundering.* • *All seam allowances are ¼",
unless otherwise specified.* • *Bindings are cut 3" wide and finish at ½". For a narrower binding, cut narrower strips.*
• *Use white sewing thread for piecing.* • *Use white quilting thread for a traditional look.*

Teddy Bear, Teddy Bear Crib Quilt

Quilt size: 50" x 64"
Finished block size: 10"

Materials

3 3/8 yards white fabric for blocks

Fat quarters or scraps of 6 to 7 different red print fabrics for pieced blocks

1 5/8 yards red solid fabric for pieced blocks and binding

3 5/8 yards backing fabric

8" x 50" piece of fabric for hanging sleeve (optional)

Batting, twin size or 58" x 72" piece

Approximately 24 skeins red embroidery floss

Cutting

From the white fabric:
Cut 12 squares, 12" x 12"
Cut 80 rectangles, 3" x 5 1/2"
Cut 4 squares, 15 1/2" x 15 1/2";
    cut in half diagonally twice,
    to make 16 triangles*

From the red print fabrics:
Cut 80 squares, 3" x 3"

From the red fabric:
Cut 20 squares, 5 1/2" x 5 1/2"
Cut 3"-wide bias strips to
    total 250"

*Note: You will use only 14 of the triangles for the sides.

Constructing the Quilt

1. For the redwork embroidery, choose six rhyming pairs of teddy bear patterns from the Patterns. Transfer the patterns to the white squares, remembering that the designs are positioned on the squares ON THE DIAGONAL.

Trace the designs onto the white fabric squares.

2. Embroider and press the blocks. Trim the pressed squares to 10 1/2" by 10 1/2", centering the design.

3. Assemble 20 patchwork blocks as shown, using the red print squares, white rectangles, and solid red squares. Press seam allowances toward the red fabric.

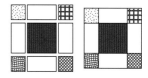

Make 20.

4. Assemble the embroidered squares, the patchwork blocks, and the white triangles as shown. Sew together in diagonal rows. Press the seams open to reduce bulk and avoid show-through of the red fabrics. Sew the rows together, pressing the seams open.

Join the blocks in diagonal rows.

Finishing

1. Cut the backing fabric into two pieces approximately 65" long. Trim the selvages off, and cut one piece in half lengthwise. Sew the narrow pieces to the sides of the wide piece. Press the seams open.

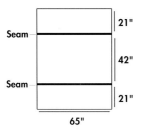

Piece the backing and press seams open.

2. Lay the quilt top right side down on a large tabletop. Trim any stray threads that might show through. Lay the batting over the top. Lay the backing over the batting, right side up. Carefully turn the quilt "sandwich" over and trim the batting and the backing to 2" larger than the quilt top on all sides.

3. Baste the three layers together by hand (or pin with safety pins if you will be machine quilting). The basting stitches or pins should be no more than 3" to 4" apart.

4. Hand or machine quilt as desired. This quilt was quilted around the colored squares.

Quilt around the red squares.

5. Trim the excess quilt top, batting, and backing, as shown. The dotted line, which connects the points of the solid red squares, is the stitching line for the binding. The solid line is the cutting line, and is 1/2" outside the stitching line.

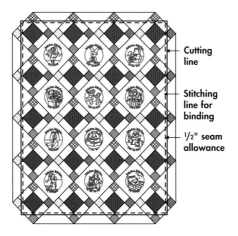

← Cutting line

← Stitching line for binding

← 1/2" seam allowance

Trim the sides of the quilt, allowing 1/2" for the binding seam allowance.

6. Sew the short ends of the bias strips together on the diagonal. Make two strips 52" long and two strips 66" long. Fold the strips in half lengthwise, wrong sides together, and press.

7. Sew the longer strips to the sides of the quilt, matching the raw edges, and using a 1/2" seam allowance. Fold the binding over the raw edges, bringing the folded edge of the binding to the back of the quilt. Hand stitch the folded edge to the backing.

8. Align the shorter strips with the top and bottom of the quilt. Fold the ends of the binding over to align with the edges of the side bindings and stitch, using a 1/2" seam allowance. Fold the binding over the raw edges and hand stitch.

Hanging Sleeve

To make a hanging sleeve for your quilt, see Adding a Hanging Sleeve on page 11.

Pillowcase

Make a sweet pillowcase with a vintage look for a coordinated crib ensemble.

1. Transfer the "Say Goodnight" pattern on page 34 to the center of a new or vintage pillowcase.

2. Embroider and press gently on a terry cloth towel.

Optional: Add lace to the pillow edge, weave a red ribbon through the openings of the lace, and tie into a bow.

TEDDY BEAR, TEDDY BEAR IRISH CHAIN QUILT

Quilt size: 51 1/2" x 51 1/2"
Finished block size: 15"

Materials

1 3/4 yards white fabric for
 blocks
1 1/8 yards light red print fabric
 for pieced blocks
1 1/4 yards red solid fabric for
 pieced blocks and binding
3 1/4 yards backing fabric
8" x 51 1/2" piece of fabric for
 hanging sleeve (optional)

Batting, twin size or 60" x 60"
 piece
Approximately 8 skeins red
 embroidery floss

Cutting

From the white fabric:
Cut 4 squares, 19" x 19"
Cut 2 strips, 3 1/2" x 42"; cut 1
 in half to make 2 short strips
Cut 4 squares, 3 1/2" x 3 1/2"
Cut 8 rectangles, 3 1/2" x 9 1/2"

From the light red print fabric:
Cut 6 strips, 3 1/2" x 42"; cut 1
 in half to make 2 short strips
Cut 40 squares, 3 1/2" x 3 1/2"

From the red fabric:
Cut 4 strips, 3 1/2" x 42"
Cut 1 strip, 3 1/2" x 21"
Cut 12 squares, 3 1/2" x 3 1/2"
Cut 6 strips, 3" x 42"; cut 2 in
 half to make 4 short strips

Constructing the Quilt

1. Choose two rhyming pairs of
teddy bear patterns from the
Patterns beginning on page 23.
Transfer the teddy bear patterns
to the white squares. Embroider
and press. Trim the squares to
15 1/2" by 15 1/2".

2. Assemble strip sets for the
five patchwork blocks. Make a
strip set by joining two red
strips, two light red print strips,
and one white strip as shown.
Press seams away from the
center. Cut the strip set into ten
units, 3 1/2" wide.

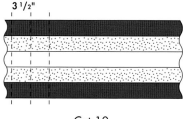

Cut 10.

3. Join three light red print strips and two red strips. Press seams toward the red. Cut ten units, 3 1/2" wide.

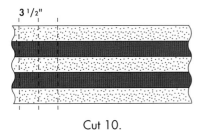

3 1/2"

Cut 10.

4. Join the half strips, two white, two print, and one red. Press seams toward the center. Cut five units 3 1/2" wide.

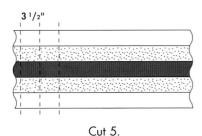

3 1/2"

Cut 5.

5. Assemble the units from Steps 2 through 4 into five blocks. Press the seams toward the center.

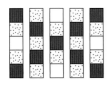

Make 5.

6. To appliqué the light red print corner squares to the embroidered blocks, fold under two adjacent edges of each square 1/4" and press. Lay one square over each corner of the embroidered blocks, wrong side of square to right side of embroidered block, matching raw edges. Hand stitch the folded edges of the square to the embroidered blocks.

Appliqué

Hand appliqué the squares on the corners of the blocks.

7. Join the five patchwork blocks and the four embroidered blocks together into three rows of three blocks as shown. Press seams away from the embroidered blocks. Sew the rows together.

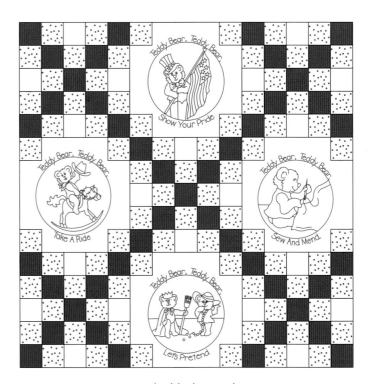

Sew the blocks together.

8. Assemble the border units as shown on the opposite page, using the red squares, light red print squares, and the white rectangles. Press seams away from the white. Sew the side border strips to the center, pressing seams toward the center. Sew the top and bottom border strips to the quilt. Press seams toward the center.

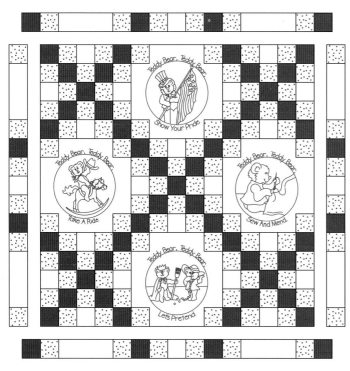

Add the border strips.

Finishing

1. Cut the backing fabric into two 1⁵/₈ yard pieces. Cut the selvages off. Follow Steps 1 through 3 for the crib quilt; see Finishing on page 14.

2. Hand or machine quilt as desired. This quilt is machine quilted in a diagonal grid as shown.

Quilt a diagonal grid by hand or machine.

3. Carefully trim the excess batting and backing even with the edge of the quilt top.

4. Join the end of each long binding strip to a short strip to make four longer strips. Press the seams open. Fold the strips in half the long way, wrong sides together, and press.

5. Sew the strips to the sides of the quilt, having right sides together and matching the raw edges. Use a ¹/₂" seam allowance, and refer to Steps 7 and 8 for the crib quilt on page 14 to finish binding your quilt. To add a hanging sleeve, see page 11.

Nursery Picture

Embroider and frame one of the blocks for a sweet decorating accessory.

Transfer one of the patterns to a 14"-square piece of white fabric. My favorites for framed pictures are "I Love You," "Say Your Prayers," and "Say Goodnight." Embroider and press. You can have it professionally framed as I did, or buy a precut mat and frame it yourself.

Teddy Bear, Teddy Bear, Sing This Song... Teddy Bear, Teddy Bear, All Year Long!

Spring Bears
Welcome All That's New.

Summer Bears
Share A Treat For Two.

Autumn Bears
Have Work To Do.

Winter Bears
Just Nap F...

...ear, Sing This Song...

TEDDY BEARS ALL YEAR

Quilt size: 37 1/2" x 37 1/2"
Finished block size: 14"

Materials

1 1/4 yards white fabric for blocks
2 fat quarters each of 4 different
   red print fabrics or scraps for
   the blocks and corner squares
5/8 yard red solid fabric for
   inner border and binding
1 1/4 yards backing fabric
8" x 37" piece of fabric for
   hanging sleeve (optional)
Batting, crib size, or 42" x 42"
   piece
Approximately 12 skeins red
   embroidery floss

Cutting

From the white fabric:
Cut 4 squares, 12" x 12"

From the red print fabrics:
Cut 8 squares, 8" x 8"; cut each
   square in half diagonally to
   make 16 triangles
Cut 4 squares, 4" x 4"

From the red fabric:
Cut 2 strips, 1 1/2" x 28 1/2"
Cut 2 strips, 1 1/2" x 30 1/2"
Cut 4 strips, 3" x 42"

Constructing the Quilt

1. Transfer the four teddy bear seasons patterns on pages 43–46 to the white squares, remembering that the designs are stitched ON THE DIAGONAL of the blocks.

Transfer the pattern to the background square.

2. Embroider the designs and press the blocks gently, right side down on a terry cloth towel. Trim the squares to 10 1/2" x 10 1/2".

3. Sew four print triangles to each embroidered block. Press seam allowances toward the red print fabric.

Sew a red print triangle to each side.

4. Sew the four blocks together to create the center of the quilt. Press seams open.

Adding the Borders

1. Mark the outline of the four 4" x 30 1/2" border strips on white fabric, but do not cut out. Transfer the border pattern on page 47 to each of the strips. Join the three pattern pieces to make the full border pattern.

2. Embroider and press. Cut out the strips on the outline.

3. Sew the 1 1/2" x 28 1/2" solid red strips to the sides of the quilt. Press seams toward the red strips. Sew the 1 1/2" x 30 1/2" red strips to the top and bottom. Press toward the red strips.

4. Sew an embroidered border to the right and left side of the quilt. Press seams toward the red border.

5. Sew the red print corner squares to the ends of the two remaining borders. Press toward the red print. Sew the borders to the top and bottom of the quilt. Press toward the red border.

Teddy Bear, Teddy Bear, Sing This Song ... Teddy Bear, Teddy Bear, All Year Long!

Spring Bears
Welcome All That's New

Summer Bears
Share A Treat For Two

Autumn Bears
Have Work To Do

Winter Bears
Just Nap Right Through!

Teddy Bear, Teddy Bear, Sing This Song ... Teddy Bear, Teddy Bear, All Year Long!

Teddy Bear, Teddy Bear, Sing This Song ... Teddy Bear, Teddy Bear, All Year Long!

Quilt
diagram

Finishing

1. Cut the backing fabric into a square, approximately 42" x 42".

2. Lay the quilt top right side down on a large tabletop. Trim any stray threads that might show through. Lay the batting over the top. Lay the quilt back over the batting, right side up. Carefully turn the quilt "sandwich" over and trim the batting and the backing to 2" larger than the quilt top.

3. Hand baste the three layers together or pin baste with safety pins.

4. Quilt by hand or machine "in the ditch" along all of the seams.

5. Carefully trim the batting and backing even with the edge of the quilt top.

6. Fold the red binding strips in half lengthwise with wrong sides together. Press.

7. Sew a strip to each side of the quilt, matching the raw edges and using a $1/2$" seam allowance. Refer to Steps 7 and 8 for the crib quilt on page 14 to finish binding your quilt.

Hanging Sleeve

To make a hanging sleeve for your quilt, see Adding a Hanging Sleeve on page 11.

VARIATIONS ON THE THEME

Innovations and adaptations using the redwork patterns

Feel free to use the designs in this book as inspiration and as a jumping-off point for limitless variations and adaptations. Rearrange or modify the patterns to suit other projects. When transferring the pattern, place elements of the design in different locations to fit the available space. The toddler's romper in the photograph at right is an example.

Appliqué

You can easily adapt many of the redwork designs in this book to appliqué. Choose designs that have few tiny shapes, eliminate the tiny shapes from the designs, or embroider the tiny shapes after the appliqué of the larger shapes is complete. See the denim jacket in the photo for a design that I appliquéd by hand. You can use your preferred appliqué technique: hand, machine, or fusible. The words and musical notes were done using the outline embroidery stitch.

Painting Redwork

Another way to interpret these redwork designs is to use fabric paint rather than embroidery stitches. Try this option when time is limited, or when the item will be receiving heavy wear.

Ballpoint fabric paint, in tubes, is ideal for these designs, as it produces a fine line of consistent thickness. This paint is available in many craft stores, and is sold under brands such as Tri-Chem, Aunt Martha's, and Liquid Embroidery. Follow product instructions for use and for care of the finished projects.

Dance/Overnight Bag

This 18" x 10" bag is just the right size for a child to carry shoes and costumes to dance class, or pajamas and a teddy bear to grandma's house.

Materials

1 yard white canvas fabric (40" wide) for bag
⅝ yard red print fabric for handles and piping trim
18" heavy-duty zipper
Transfer paper
1 tube of red fabric paint with built-in ballpoint

Cutting

From the white canvas:
Cut 2 circles, 11" in diameter
Cut 1 rectangle, 19" x 35"

From the red print:
Cut 2 strips, 6" x 34"
Cut 2 strips, 2" x 35"

Paint the Redwork

Transfer the "Turn Around" pattern on page 23 (for dance bag), or "Say Goodnight" pattern on page 34 (for overnight bag) to the center of the circles, using the transfer/tracing paper. Paint the designs with ballpoint fabric paint.

Prepare the Bag and Handles

1. With right sides together, baste the short edges of the 19" x 35" piece of canvas together, using a ½" seam allowance, to make a tube. Press the seam open.

2. Center and pin the zipper to the wrong side of the basted seam. Sew the edges of the zipper to the canvas, using a zipper foot. Remove the basting.

3. Fold each 6" red print strip in half lengthwise, right sides together, and stitch ½" from the long raw edges. Turn the tubes right side out, and press flat.

4. Tie a knot in the middle of each handle. Trim the ends to a 45° angle.

5. Pin the ends of the handles 4" down from the zipper on the raw edges of the bag tube. Tack the handle to the bag, approximately 4" from the raw edges of the handle, stitching and backstitching several times with your machine, or use a satin stitch.

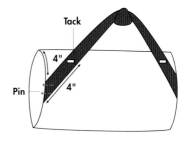

Pin the handle to the bag and tack it by machine.

Prepare the Trim

Fold one long edge of each 2" red print strip under ½" and press. Using a ½" seam allowance, join the short ends of each strip, having right sides together, to create a "circle." Press the seam open.

Assemble the Bag

1. With wrong sides together, match the raw edges of one "embroidered" circle to the raw edges on one end of the bag tube. Be sure that the design is oriented vertically between the handles. Pin, and machine baste, using a ½" seam allowance. Repeat for the other circle.

2. Pin the long, unfolded raw edge of a trim strip to the raw edge of the bag ends, right sides together. Sew, using a ½" seam allowance.

3. Fold the trim strip over so that the folded edge of the strip meets the seamline on the circle and encloses the seam allowances. Hand sew the folded edge in place.

4. Fill the bag with dance shoes or pajamas, and you're off!

Teddy Bear, Teddy Bear,
Read The News.

27

31

Teddy Bear, Teddy Bear,

Put Out The Light.

34

Teddy Bear, Teddy Bear, Show Your Pride.

Teddy Bear, Teddy Bear, Let's Pretend.

40

A1　Join to A2.

B1　Join to B2.

Teddy Bear, Teddy Bear,

Sing This Song . . . Teddy Bear,

Teddy Bear, All Year Long!

Teddy Bear,

B2　Join to B1.

A2　Join to A1.

47

ABOUT THE AUTHOR

Jan Rapacz is a dedicated needleworker. She loves to experiment with every needlework technique she comes across, and has spent countless late nights with her needle, long after her two young daughters and dear husband have gone to bed.

Jan learned to love needlework from her mother and grandmother, and feels grateful that their knowledge was handed down. She has taught classes in smocking, tatting, and silk ribbon embroidery; she feels that teaching is a responsibility of any needleworker who wants to keep the techniques from becoming lost arts.

In addition to her work on this book, Jan has had smocking patterns and embroidery designs published in *Sew Beautiful* magazine and tatting designs published in *Workbasket*.

Collecting vintage linens, quilts, and clothing, especially those with fine embroidery, is a passion for Jan. Her frequent visits to antique stores provide both inspiration for needlework designs and additions to her collection.

For information about other C&T titles write for a free catalog:
C&T Publishing, Inc.
P.O. Box 1456
Lafayette, CA 94549
(800) 284-1114
e-mail: ctinfo@ctpub.com
website: www.ctpub.com

For quilting supplies:
Cotton Patch Mail Order
3405 Hall Lane, Dept. CTB
Lafayette, CA 94549
(800) 835-4418
(925) 283-7883
email: quiltusa@yahoo.com
website: www.quiltusa.com